# Lord, Deliver Me From Me

## HOW TO STOP BECOMING YOUR OWN WORST ENEMY

### Dr. Brenda Stratton

This is Dr.Brenda Stratton contact information:
drbstratton@me.com, www.messagetothenations.org,
757-277-9714 P.O. BOX 2694 Chesapeake, VA 23327

Produced by:

FriesenPress
Suite 300 — 852 Fort Street
Victoria, BC, Canada V8W 1H8

www.friesenpress.com

Distributed to the trade by The Ingram Book Company

# Table of Contents

# Dedication

This book is dedicated first to my Heavenly Father for His love and faithful support toward me. This book is also dedicated in loving memory of my Mother Amanda Stratton who was my biggest supporter and encourager in life.

# Foreword

## John Dawson

President Emeritus,
Youth With A Mission International

BRILLIANTLY SIMPLE, BUT SURPRISINGLY POWERFUL, I found this to be one of the most practical, helpful books I have ever read. Written with wisdom, love and authenticity, there is nothing superfluous here. In each chapter, Brenda alludes to her own dramatic story; just enough to illustrate something truly important, candid enough to elicit from us an equally honest appraisal of our own story.

Brenda respects us, seems to know us, takes us forthrightly by the hand and leads us to healing, restoration, freedom, dignity and fulfilling purpose. She tells us what to do in plain language; every chapter has us acting immediately. If we don't know what to believe, or to choose, or to say, or to pray, she lays it out simply, even putting the words in our mouth if we feel inadequate.

This is a handbook for every believer, written by a veteran missionary who is a pillar of integrity and a great inspiration to the spiritual leaders who know her.

## Pastor Dan Backens

Pastor of New Life Providence Church
Virginia

I HAVE HAD THE PRIVILEGE OF BEING BRENDA STRATTON'S pastor for the last few years and have seen her minister to people in a variety of settings and so I can attest, "Brenda is the real deal." She is a woman of remarkable gifts — she has been a missionary, teacher, preacher, ordained minister, and a successful leader in church and parachurch organizations, yet, with all her accomplishments she is not a woman who is vain or proud. Brenda is truly a humble servant of the Lord who has a proven track record and character with her only desire to please Jesus.

Her book, *Lord Deliver Me from Me,* is a short but meaty book that will inspire biblical hope and healing for whoever reads it. *Lord Deliver Me from Me* is a wonderful combination of Brenda's own spiritual journey, poignant stories of others, a lot of Scripture and insightful and relevant applications. This book would be ideal for small groups, discipleship classes or for personal devotions. Brenda writes in a very accessible way — both young and old alike will be blessed by her words.

I really appreciate the topics Brenda has selected for her book. Each chapter touches on issues that everyone can relate to such as overcoming fear, anger and rejection. Every page is full of nuggets of truth that are life-changing if received and applied by faith. There is an unmistakable anointing that emanates from her words — I believe it is the power of the Holy Spirit.

Brenda has experienced some pain and setback in her life and has found Christ and His Word to be more than enough. When it comes to the things of God, she is a practitioner not a theorist. She truly is a walking testimony to the message of her book.

Are you ready to 'get out of your own way' and 'let God do what He promised He will do'? My sister and friend, Brenda Stratton, can lead you gently into true freedom and wholeness. I thank God for her and her message.

## Pastor Richard Heard

Pastor of Christian Tabernacle Church
Houston, Texas

SOMEONE HAS SAID, AND NOT NECESSARILY TONGUE IN cheek either, that 96% of families are dysfunctional and the other 4% are so dysfunctional they won't talk about it. The human race began with one family and even a casual reading of their account in Genesis reveals how incredibly dysfunctional they were from the beginning. The truth is that we are a fallen race, who live in a fallen world that is ruled by a fallen lord! In this world, you don't get by without becoming wounded.

Fortunately for us, the gospel is all about God's desire to heal mankind where he is broken. Oh, how He loves us! The problem is knowing how to appropriate the healing He has already graciously provided and made available to us! Healing is often a process. We all wish it would happen instantly, perhaps at our conversion, but that is generally only where healing begins.

In *Deliver Me From Me*, Brenda tells us how to go about this process of finding healing and helpfully illuminates this experience by candidly sharing with us her own journey. As a traveler who is familiar with this road down which healing will take us, hers is not the impractical advice of one who only has theories to offer. Rather it is the sound counsel of someone who has been down this way herself and who knows well the road we are on.

Having known Brenda for many years and having enjoyed the opportunity to work with her in ministry, I can tell you that she genuinely cares about helping people. This book proves it by telling us how to resolve the inner struggles that bring so many of us pain. It will bless you.

# Deliver Me from Me

# Preface

AS I WAS driving MY CAR ONE DAY, I CLEARLY HEARD THE Lord say to me, "I want you to write a book called *Deliver Me from Me.*" I had been struggling over writing a book and now I had His clear direction. This is that book. *Deliver Me from Me* is the story of my journey and the transformation of my soul.

After more than thirty years of ministering to people in the area of life transformation (inner healing and deliverance), one of the major issues that kept resurfacing was the area of unforgiveness. We are often our greatest hindrance to gaining the freedom we want in our lives.

I have had the privilege of ministering to thousands of people in individual counseling sessions and with their permission, I have included some of their stories.

Perhaps the greatest gift God has given us is the ability to forget. If we were to remember all of our painful experiences, disappointments, and shame in our conscious everyday life, we would go crazy. So we bury those painful experiences without ever dealing with them and later on in life, they come up at the most inopportune times to affect us. Every experience we have ever had has contributed to molding our personalities and making us act the way we do.

> *Inner healing does not erase the memory or change our personal history. Rather, it enables us to cherish even the worst moments in our lives, for through them God has inscribed eternal lessons on to our hearts and prepared us to minister to all who have suffered in the same way.* (John and Paula Sandford, *The Transformation of the Inner Man*)

Believe it or not, you will bless someone one day with what you've experienced, *if you allow God to heal you.* God wants to turn your **mess** into your **message**, and your **tests** will become your **testimony**.

Getting back to the car, God began to show me that *I was my biggest problem.*

We sometimes want to blame everybody else — family members, spouse, children, friends, and even the devil. Situations, people, and the devil have certainly affected our lives, but most of the time it is really our own selves that get in the way of us fulfilling our destinies.

I was in full-time ministry and Spirit-filled, but I could not thank God for giving me life. I never wanted to be here. I just didn't appreciate life and more so, *my* life. I knew I wasn't supposed to feel this way but I didn't know why I did.

Many years ago, I began to ask, *Why do I act like this?*

God began to show me that in my mother's womb, I received a spirit of rejection. She just didn't want another child. I was the youngest of three children, with a five-year gap between my sister and me. My mother had thought that she was through having children. She went to two doctors in the same day, and both told her she was pregnant.

In order for my life to flourish, I had to stop those negative thought patterns in my life and get rid of the strongholds that bound me to the past, such as unforgiveness, anger, resentment, bitterness, anxiety, and fears.

*Lord, deliver me from wrong thinking, from my lack of understanding, from getting in the way of what You want to do in my life.*

**Lord, deliver me from me!**

# Introduction

I AM GRATEFUL FOR THE MANY PEOPLE FROM WHOM I HAVE gleaned information on this subject. The reason I'm writing this book is to show you just how practically God wants to transform our lives in the process and how He goes about doing that.

You will be taking a journey with the Holy Spirit to uncover areas where God wants to bring healing in your life. The inner healing and deliverance process is what I call, "life transformation process." It's where the Holy Spirit goes through the pages of our lives and uncovers issues that are still bothering us, beginning the process of inner healing.

John and Paula Sandford define inner healing as "the process of prayer and counsel for sanctification and transformation." It is a ministry within the body of Christ to enable believers to come to a more effective and continual death on the cross. These challenges include sickness of emotions, which is generally caused by what has been done to us.

*Lord, deliver me from me!* Deliver me from wrong thinking, from my lack of understanding, from getting in the way of what You want to do in my life.

Satan does come to deceive us and lie to us but what we do with these lies and deception is what determines the outcome of our lives. Jesus not only defeated the enemy at the cross, but also gave us the power to live a holy life through the power of the Holy Spirit living inside of us.

Remember — the enemy comes to rob, steal, kill, and destroy, and he waits for an opportunity to take advantage of the situation.

## The Importance of the Cross and the Power of the Blood

The cross and the shed blood of Jesus is the central theme for every person who comes to God for healing. Without Jesus' provision to us through His blood, death, and resurrection, there would be no freedom from sin, forgiveness of sin, healing, or victorious Christian living. All provision comes from the work that Jesus did on the cross by dying in our places. He made it possible for you and me to be made whole.

Life transformation is not possible without the cross of Jesus Christ and the shedding of His blood. The cross represents Jesus restoring us back to our Heavenly Father (Papa) and restoring wholeness in spirit, soul, and body.

Throughout this book you will be asked to activate your will to cooperate with what Jesus has done for you already. The Christian life is always a cooperative effort between you and the Holy Spirit, to receive what Jesus has already provided. God offers to you and gives you the grace to participate in what He has done and is doing.

Just as salvation is offered to all but not all take advantage of the gift, we must take advantage of receiving our lives' transformation. God never takes away our responsibility to participate in our wholeness.

Get ready as we go on a personal journey of unveiling pain, unforgiveness, and the lies you have been told about your identity and self through circumstances, family, friends, and others.

## Prayer of Healing

*Lord, as I begin this healing process, I ask that You deliver me from all the things that are holding me back from my future destiny. I take responsibility by activating my spirit and soul--that is my mind, will and emotions. I give permission to the Holy Spirit to walk back through my life and find the areas from which I need to be delivered and healed. Let all the hidden secret things be revealed.*

*I open myself up to Jesus, the power of the cross, and His blood to bring forth this healing in my life. Thank You, Lord, for opening my eyes where I have been blind. Thank You for loving and accepting me just as I am, yet loving me too much to let me stay as I am.*

*In Jesus' Name, Amen.*

## Questions

1. Ask yourself why you react in a certain way.
2. Is the Holy Spirit bringing up a memory of a pain in your life while you wait before Him?
3. Is there a nagging memory, disappointment, or emotional pain that you can't seem to be able to get over?
4. When was the first time you experienced this pain or hurt?

## Application

1. Go to a quiet place and listen to God's soft prompting. Wait for the Holy Spirit to show you the area with which He wants you to deal.
2. Write out what He shows you and allow Him to minister His loving, healing powers to you.

# Chapter 1

## FORGIVING MY FATHER

FORGIVING MY FATHER BEGAN THE JOURNEY OF GOD healing my heart. God took me by the hand and began to show me the emotional scars in my life.

I knew there was something wrong with me, but I didn't know how to fix it. I read books on inner healing, emotional hurts and pain, and even went to seminars to find out anything that would help me alleviate my pain. God was gentle with me, going through issues in my life that hurt me.

My father was emotionally bankrupt. He was a very strict, domineering, and authoritarian person. If he said the sky was purple and you didn't agree with him, there would be a big argument in the house. He was an excellent provider, but he did not give emotional support. I felt I could never be good enough to get his approval; I was always seeking his support and approval.

I didn't come from perfect parents. My parents had their own issues, hurts, disappointments, and pain—which in turn came from them not having perfect parents.

> *Adding up two parents, four grandparents, eight great grandparents, and sixteen great-great-grandparents, gives a total of thirty people! Thirty human beings within a mixture of fleshly and godly desires, actions, beliefs, stumbling, falls, and besetting sins, have passed their iniquity on to each of us. If there has been divorce and remarriage or adoption of children, even more people within four generations are involved. The greater tragedy, however, is that our parents also each had thirty people whose sin affected them, and four grandparents each had thirty people, etc.* (Chester and Betsy Kylstra, *Restoring the Foundations*, p.123)

Just think about this. Everything we have experienced in life — our background, experiences, and pain — have affected us in some way, both negative and positive.

When I learned that my parents did the best with what they had to work with in their own lives; that enabled me to forgive my father and release him. He could not give me what he did not have. I could not move on in life *until I forgave him.*

When I forgave him, a *brightness and lightness* came over me.

A father plays such a significant role in his daughter's life. If we don't get this issue straight, we will continue to look for approval from a man and look for love in all the wrong places. We usually gather the first understanding of our Heavenly Father's characteristics by looking at our earthly fathers. What we get most of the time is a distorted concept of who God is and what He looks like.

If you had a father, stepfather, mother, stepmother or other significant adult who disappointed you, belittled you, broke your heart, and made you feel like an orphan, *forgive him/her, and release him/her to God.* This is the first step toward your journey of healing. You can't be delivered from yourself until you have forgiven your past and moved on.

In order for my life to flourish, I had to stop those negative thought patterns in my life and get rid of the strongholds that bound me to the past such as forgiveness, anger, resentment, bitterness, anxiety and fears.

*Lord, deliver me from wrong thinking, from my lack of understanding, from getting in the way of what You want to do in my life.*

## Prayer of Healing

*Heavenly Father, I bring to the foot of the cross all of my pain and disappointments, rejection, abandonment, and abuse that I experienced through the hands of my father/mother. By an act of my will, I choose to forgive my earthly daddy/mommy for all the pain and suffering he/she caused me. All of the pain is wiped away through the finished work of Jesus and His blood on the cross.*

*I forgive you daddy/mommy for not showing me love, for rejection, abandonment, abuse, and for failing to show me what Father God looks like. I forgive you and release you in Jesus' Name, Amen.*

## Questions

1. What was your relationship like with your father, or the significant male who acted as a parent figure toward you?

2. What memories do you have of your father that cause you to feel bad or cry?
3. What was your relationship like with your mother, or significant female who acted as a parent figure toward you?
4. What memories do you have of your mother that cause you to feel bad or cry?

## Application

1. Imagine your father/mother before you and forgive them for each of the offenses (specifically) that you still feel pain over.
2. Ask God to wash away the pain of each memory through the blood of Jesus Christ.

# Chapter 2

## FORGIVING MYSELF

*BROKEN RELATIONSHIPS, HURTS, PAIN, DISAPPOINTMENTS, friends who didn't like me...*

One of the greatest hindrances to fulfilling our destinies is our inability to forgive. It is not what happened to us that really affects us the most, but our perception of the incident. Instead of looking at God and who He is, we spend time focusing on the person who offended us, and become like them.

*Why become like the person who offended you?*

God made us with the capacity to love Him with all our hearts, souls, and minds. We only have one emotional focus and it should be *focusing our attention on loving God.* We become what we look upon the most. It takes time and energy to keep revisiting the offense that someone has done to us.

*But time is too precious.*

In the days of the Roman Empire, if a person killed another, the dead body was strapped to the body of the one who killed him. Over time, the decay of the dead body would begin to seep through the pores of the one who carried it. It would eventually poison the person carrying the body, and he would die.

Living in unforgiveness is like strapping the unforgiven person to you. The poison of holding him will eventually seep into your own life and poison you. When you hold onto unforgiveness, you are spiritually tied to the very thing that you hate. ***Forgiveness is setting the other person free so that you can also be free.***

*Forgiveness releases both parties.* Sometimes, the party with whom you are angry, in this present situation, might be tied to someone in your past that you have never forgiven, and you are reminded of him.

One of the greatest healing moments in my life was when I listed all the things that I didn't like about myself and the hurts that I had caused to others and myself. I somehow felt that I didn't measure up. I went through the list and said to God, *"You forgive me, Father and I forgive myself."*

I expressed how I felt, and God listened.

*I waited patiently for the Lord; he inclined to me and heard my cry. He drew me up from the pit of destruction, out of the miry bog, and set my feet upon a rock, making my steps secure. Psalms 40:1-2, ESV*

## Prayer of Healing

*Father I thank You that Your Word says in 1 John 1:9, "If we confess our sins You are faithful and just to forgive us our sins and to cleanse us from all unrighteousness." Because You have forgiven me so much, I choose to forgive myself for all the pain*

*that I have caused to myself and others. I will no longer hold these sins as debts in my life. Thank You for Your forgiveness.*
*In Jesus' Name, Amen.*

Write down all the areas in your life for which you want to be forgiven. After writing them down, cross each one out and write, *"God forgives me, and I forgive myself."*

This is the time to be really specific and ask the Holy Spirit to reveal all those areas that you are holding over your head — the things that you feel are wrong about yourself and for which you just can't seem to forgive yourself.

## Questions

1. What are the past sins, character flaws or mistakes that still trouble you, from which you seem not to find freedom?
2. What lie has the enemy told you about yourself?
3. What is the truth from the Word of God about you?

## Application

1. Write out your new truth that God has shown you from His Word.
2. Declare this Word over and over during the day, getting it in your spirit.

# Chapter 3

## FORGIVING DIFFICULT PEOPLE

IN MY MANY YEARS OF MINISTRY, I HAVE FOUND THAT THE greatest need in life is the need for forgiveness. We just don't want to let go of some issues. Often we don't know how these issues are affecting us in our present situations, and as individuals, we aren't able to deal with too much at a time.

I remember early in my Christian life when I talked to the Lord and said, "I'm tired of dealing with this stuff over and over. Let's get it all straight NOW."

As I went to prayer, the Lord said, "You can't."

"Why not?" I said.

"Because you couldn't handle it right now," He continued.

God is so wonderful. He gives us just what we can deal with at one time. Forgiveness is a lifelong practice.

I had to forgive someone in authority. He was constantly critical of my work and demanding; I couldn't do anything to please him. My friends and family didn't like the way he was treating me. It was hard to forgive him, as I had once held him in high esteem. I had looked up to him as an exemplary, godly leader.

God said to me, "You cannot move out of this job until you have forgiven him."

The Lord began to show me how to forgive him and release honor to the office he held. From God's point of view, even when the person is unreasonable and demanding, you can forgive him, release him, and take it to the cross.

Naming the offense is important because it closes the door to the offense. It is like peeling an onion one layer at a time. *My unforgiveness came off layer by layer.*

**Forgiveness is a process** and it doesn't happen overnight. It needs to be worked through and God has to give you the right perspective. We can honor the position, even when the person is wrong. God moved me from that position only when I was able to forgive him. After I forgave him, God released me and provided a new job that led into a new business.

Ask the Holy Spirit to bring to your remembrance anyone you need to forgive; this can include people living or deceased. Just because the person is deceased doesn't mean it is over. Remember, **forgiveness is more for you than for the other person.**

Write down all the names of the people you need to forgive and their offenses.

You may be saying, "Wait just a minute. Do I also have to think about the offense he or she committed?"

Yes, because the more specific you are, the freer you will become. After you have composed your list, repeat this prayer of healing for every name and the offense.

Take all of these hurts and pains, and put them at the foot of the cross, where Jesus washes them away with his blood.

*As far as the east is from the west, so far has He removed our transgressions from us. Psalm 103:12*

## Prayer of Healing

*Father, I thank You that You have made it possible for me to experience freedom through forgiveness. The way to receive forgiveness is to give forgiveness. I forgive _____(name) for _____ (offense). I forgive him/her for hurting me and causing me pain. I release him from any debt I thought he owed me. I also let go of trying to get even or judging him.*

*I placed them in the hands of Jesus and His work on the Cross. Therefore the blood of Jesus washes me clean.*

*In Jesus' Name, Amen.*

Naming the offense is important because it closes the door to the offense. You may have to forgive a person for multiple offenses in order to complete the healing process. Depending on the severity of the hurt, it may require more time to forgive.

What does forgiveness feel like? You will know you have forgiven these people when you can recall their names without feeling pain in your heart or the desire for revenge. You will know you have forgiven them when you can freely pray for them and speak blessings over their lives. You still want the best for them even though they are not part of your inner circle of friends.

## Questions

1. List all the names of those you need to forgive.
2. After you have listed all the names you can think of, ask the Holy Spirit if there is anyone else you need to forgive.

## Application

1. Forgive each person on your list, including each and every offense.
2. Pray a prayer of blessing over them.

# Chapter 4

## WHEN YOU ARE NEVER
## GOOD ENOUGH

*"I'M SO STUPID. I WILL NEVER GET ANYTHING RIGHT." "WHY can't you be like your sister or your brother? They're so much smarter than you." "If I make a mistake I will be punished by God." "God doesn't love me the way He loves others."*

Poison thoughts...

Negative thoughts, stinking thinking, ungodly beliefs, lies from the enemy (Satan). We all need to get rid of them. We have thoughts that don't really belong to us, which have helped formulate who we think we are. These thoughts usually come from childhood experiences, from those in authority over us, or those who had influence over us. We buy into the lie that these thoughts tell us who we are. We allow them to play over and over in our minds, without ever examining whether these things are really true about us.

My father said to me, "You are going to college, but you are stupid."

I bought into these thoughts and got through life in college, barely making it through on my grades.

The change came when I saw myself differently. I began to tell myself that I could graduate in three and half years, if I did twenty credits per semester. I told myself that I was getting all A's, and I began to speak that into my life. I chose to believe that "*I could do all things through Christ who strengthens me.*" (Philippians 4:13)

My friends and teachers laughed at me.

I studied hard and I got all A's. I graduated in three and half years and I was on the dean's list. With my grades, I was able to get a scholarship for graduate school.

***The Word of God is the most powerful evicting agent you can use.*** If the thoughts didn't come from God, you don't want them circling around in your head. Let's take back our minds by evicting all intruders.

> "*We use our powerful God-tools for smashing warped philosophies, tearing down barriers erected against the truth of God, and fixing every loose thought and emotion and impulse into the structure of life shaped by Christ.*" 2 Corinthians 10:5, MSG.

Get into a quiet place and close your eyes. Begin to allow the Holy Spirit to show you the most damaging thoughts. Write those thoughts down. For each of these negative thoughts, replace it with something positive. (For example, you have been saying, "I'm so dumb I can't master this." Replace that thought with this: "*With God's help I am able to do all things through Christ who strengthens me.*")

If you need help in writing out positive statements about yourself, read the Bible — especially the books of Ephesians, Philippians, and Colossians — and see what God has to say about who you are in Him.

## Prayer of Healing

*Heavenly Father, forgive me for believing these negative thoughts about myself. I renounce and break agreement with that thought _____ (Name out that thought), and I replace it with this new thought _____ (Name the new thought out). Thank You for forgiving me and releasing me from these negative thoughts through the power of the cross and the Blood of Jesus.*

*In Jesus' Name, Amen.*

You will never be good enough if you listen to the lie of the enemy because he is always distorting your identity to derail you from your destiny.

## Questions

1. What lies have you believed about yourself? Write them out.
2. Ask the Holy Spirit to show you what His truth is concerning the lie you believed. (Write out His statement of truth)

## Application

1. Speak out new truth about yourself so that your spirit can increase and give you power over the negative influences in your life.

*They triumphed over him by the blood of the Lamb and by the word of their testimony. (Referring to Satan) Revelation 12:11a*

# Chapter 5

## OVERCOMING FEAR

*"I CANNOT DO THIS BY MYSELF." "I AM NOT QUALIFIED TO DO this and it requires more skills than I have."*

Have you ever let fear grip you so much that you became paralyzed?

I remember a time when I allowed fear to stop me from doing what God had called me to do. It was so dark, I felt like I was in a deep hole. I got my eyes off of God, and started to look at the "cannot" and the "am not." Instead of looking at God and His ability to work through me, I looked at what I thought I couldn't do.

Fear can stop you from accomplishing your dreams and vision.

I had the fear of failing and fear of speaking to large groups of people. I was often so nervous and afraid that people wouldn't accept what I was saying or would laugh at or make fun of me that I was paralyzed with fear.

God said to me, *"Be not afraid of their faces: for I am with thee to deliver thee, saith the Lord."* Jeremiah 1:8

I learned that God would give me the grace and courage to speak; I had to believe in myself.

I joined the drama team and started speaking before groups of people. People clapped and applauded when I took the stage. As I saw success, I began to believe that I could do this and people would listen. I found my voice when I did comedy. I went on to win the Most Convincing and Most Persuasive Speech Award at Harbor College in Wilmington, California.

It takes courage to do the things that you feel you are destined to do. God always gives you an assignment that is bigger than you. He would never get the credit if it were something that you could do all by yourself from your box of tools. *God gives us His assignment and His tools to do it.*

You are the greatest hindrance to reaching your goals. It is your beliefs and perspectives of the situation that are standing in your way--not your spouse, parents, friends, or those in authority over you.

I like this definition of courage: *"In spite of fear, I will do this action anyway."*

It doesn't mean that you don't experience the fear, but you can determine that you are going to do this through God's help.

The best illustration of this in Scripture is when we see Peter get out of that boat and walk on water. He didn't determine first that the task was too great and that no human being could really walk on water. He just got out of that boat and walked to Jesus. As long as his eyes were focused upon Jesus, he did not fail. But the minute he took his eyes off Jesus, he started sinking.

Is there is a dream or vision you know you're supposed to fulfill? Have you allowed fear to grip your heart?

Now get that dream and vision in mind. Write out three action points that you will start implementing this week. Start with one today!

## Prayer of Healing

*Father, I thank You for this enormous task that You have entrusted to me. It is not based on my capabilities; it is based on Your abilities, which You will work through me. I thank You for trusting me with this task while I cooperate with You to see it accomplished. Thank You for the courage to begin, because Your Word says, "I can do all things through Jesus Christ, who strengthens me."*

*In Jesus' Name, Amen.*

## Questions

1. What is the dream that you have let go of and feel it's too late to accomplish?
2. What are the steps you will make today toward making your dream come true?
3. The Bible says nothing is impossible with God. Why are you still afraid?

## Application

Write out three action points and start implementing them this week.

1. Get an accountability person to pray with you and help keep you on target.

# Chapter 6

## ANGRY AT GOD

*"WHY WEREN'T YOU THERE FOR ME GOD? I DEPENDED ON YOU and you failed me."*

Are you angry with God? Was there something you wanted him to do and He didn't come through for you?

A failed marriage, a loved one died...and you blamed God.

You know you're not supposed to be angry with God but you still feel angry about your life...and you blame God.

It's like the play *Your Arm's Too Short to Box with God.* You know it doesn't do you any good to argue, blame, or be angry with God, but we do it anyway. We don't want to admit that we are really angry with God.

Cindy (not her real name) was sexually exploited and abused by her father from the time she was six years old. Her mother did not protect her and Cindy also became angry with God for not protecting her. Cindy soon got involved in abusive relationships. She had low self-esteem and attracted abusive boyfriends. As a single mother, Cindy perpetuated her anger onto her child. She screamed and hit the child, because she was angry at life.

Cindy eventually sought help. She took steps to walk through inner healing and deliverance from her original pain — her anger at God for allowing her to grow up in a family with an abusive father and an unprotective mother. *God met her in a deep and personal way.* **His grace and mercy was always there for her.** When she learned that He didn't approve of the situation, she could forgive her perpetrator. Her parents hadn't had the skills or the ability to love her or nurture her.

*God's mercy, love, and grace were always there.*

**Forgiveness was more for her.** Cindy began to see her daughter in a different light and became kinder to her.

Psalms 139 says, "God has planned out each day of our lives." He has a destiny and a direction that He wants us to go. The ironic thing is that He has given us a free will to choose His way or our way.

Many times, the places we find ourselves in are the result of the choices we have made. There is no pat answer here, but following God's plan is the best way. After I get through fussing with God, there are two choices — *His plan or my plan.*

It doesn't do any good to "box" with God because in the end, you won't win. It is true, "Father knows best."

If you remain angry with God, you will never be able to see His goodness toward you, because you will be looking through lenses that are colored with blame and despair. *Forgive God, as this will bring healing to your life.* **Forgiveness is always more for you.** Remember God already knows what is in your heart. He just wants you to talk to Him openly and honestly, NO FAKE FACE! He can deal with honesty, not hypocrisy.

We sometimes do not want to admit that we are really angry with God because we feel ashamed, and if we speak it out loud, He will punish us and our situation will get worse.

Psalms 142 says, *I cried out to the Lord for the Lord's mercy. I poured out my complaints before Him and told Him all my troubles.* Remember that you are the creation, and He is still the creator. If you were looking from His perspective, you might do the same thing. We can pour out our complaints before God.

## Questions

1. What are you angry with God about?

## Application

1. Talk to God openly and honestly about your complaint.
2. Sit long enough for Him to give you His perspective about it.

# Chapter 7

## WHEN YOU NEED TO MOVE
## ON FROM TOXIC PEOPLE

HAVE YOU EVER HAD TOXIC PEOPLE IN YOUR LIFE THAT didn't add to you, but drained you?

I had a friend who was someone I looked up to. But whenever I shared with her about what I was doing, she always had a negative comment to make. She wouldn't encourage me in what I was doing. She was a perfectionist and a control freak. Every time I left her presence, I would feel bad about myself and unsure if I had done the right thing. It was difficult, but what I saw was that I valued her opinion more than I valued God.

I soon became less dependent on her for her advice and opinion. We started talking less and less and became more distant from one another. Sometimes the Lord will move these people out from your life.

Toxic people always put you down. Even when you accomplish something good, they don't compliment you, or they tell you could do a better job. They remain critical of you. They are people that you don't want in your inner circle because they help formulate what you believe about yourself and your world. When we place people in such high esteem in our lives, we focus more on what they have to say about us, than what God says about us. When they become an "idol" in our lives, their word becomes the bottom line instead of God.

Birds of a feather flock together. Don't hang around with toxic people because you will take on the characteristics of those you hang around with.

God encouraged me through His Word.

*In the year that King Uzziah died, I saw the Lord, high and exalted, seated on a throne; and the train of his robe filled the temple. Isaiah 6:1 NIV*

What He showed me was that I had my eyes on a person more than on Him. If you focus on man, you become like man. *Focus on God and you will become Christ-like.*

Look around and see if there are toxic people in your life. Now is the time to release them and let them go. This does not mean that you do not love them or pray for them. Continue to love them and wish the very best for them but don't let their toxic nature or critical words get into your heart.

Ask the Lord if there are relationships in your life that need to be altered. You need to release them, let them go, and stop the influence they have in your life.

## Prayer of Healing

*Heavenly Father, show me who are the toxic relationships in my life. Let all hidden things be revealed so that I may know whom it is that You want me to connect with and who not to connect with.*

*Father, forgive me for allowing certain people to become idols in my life. I repent for this. It is You and only You that has the final say-so over who I am and who I will become. I take these people and I place them at the foot of the cross through the blood of Jesus Christ's forgiving and releasing them.*

*In Jesus' Name, Amen.*

There are so many circumstances in our lives that we cannot change, but it is important to change what is destroying us. There are difficult people whom we can't get out of our lives. We can consider them the "spiritual sandpaper" of our lives. They are there to help smooth out the rough areas in our character and make us look more like Jesus. We need to move away from toxic people, in order to move on in life.

## Questions

1. Who are people you need to move on from?
2. Where is your identity coming from?
3. What does God say about you?

## Application

1. Make it a practice to declare what God says about you (instead of what others say about you).
2. Take steps to move away from those "toxic people" you listed.

# Chapter 8

## KICK DISAPPOINTMENTS
## OUT OF YOUR LIFE

I HAD THE DESIRE TO GET MARRIED AND HAVE A FAMILY BUT it did not materialize in the manner I chose. I was disappointed with God for quite a long time because He did not seem to answer the one desire I wanted fulfilled.

One of the biggest disappointments in life is when we have an expectation of something that does not manifest in the timing or manner we want. These disappointments sometimes lead to depression and a loss of hope.

*Hope deferred makes the heart sick but a longing fulfilled is a tree of life.* Proverbs 13:12 NASB

*Delight yourself in the Lord; And He will give you the desires of your heart. Psalm 37:4, NASB*

An unfulfilled desire, however, can make you feel desperate, and you want to help God by answering your own prayer.

I prayed all kind of prayers, spoke the Word, did everything I knew to do as a Christian, but to no avail; that prayer wasn't answered in my timing. One thing I really didn't do was surrender my requests into His hand and totally give Him permission to direct my life in that area. There was really no peace in that part of my life, until I surrendered that portion to God. *Please deliver me from me, Lord!*

We sometimes have areas in our lives that we keep to ourselves and we won't even let God touch them — whether it's God's plan for our life or not, we become determined to get what we want.

Take a good hard look at your life. Are there some areas that you haven't totally surrendered to God?

If you want to kick disappointments out of your life, **your expectations must be in line with what He desires.** *Lord, not my will but Your will be done.*

> *Roll your works upon the Lord (commit and trust them wholly to Him; He will cause your thoughts to become agreeable to His will, and) so shall your plans be established and succeed.* Proverbs 16:3 AMP

## Prayer of Healing

*Lord, I admit I have some areas in my life where I have expectations of You, even though they may not be according to Your will. I ask You to forgive me for taking the reins of my life and dictating to You what's best for me. This life is supposed to be a cooperation between You and me. I give You permission to change and rearrange any right or expectation I have set up as more important than You. I make You Lord of my expectations. Thank You, for You truly know best.*

*In Jesus' Name. Amen.*

## Question

1. What are your disappointments and unrealized expectations?

## Application

1. List all your disappointments and expectations.
2. Surrender each one of these disappointments and expectations to God for His approval.
3. Give God opportunity to show you what He desires for your life.

# Chapter 9

## EMBRACING GOD,
## MY FATHER

THE GREATEST REVELATION I HAVE EVER HAD IN MY LIFE
was finding out that God was truly my Father. He just wasn't
God up in the sky or Jesus in my heart. He was God, my
Father. Whatever kind of father you have, you might have
placed his characteristics on your heavenly Father. That is
just what I did.

For me, having the concept of God as my heavenly Father
was only an intellectual assent. But the day I understood that
God was my biggest fan and that He truly loved me uncon-
ditionally changed my very life.

I remember a time in prayer when He began to pour His
love on me. The first time I experienced this, was at a prayer
meeting. God began to say, *"I love you, I love you, I love
you,"* over and over.

This was the first time I heard God say, "I love you,
Brenda. **I've covered you with my love."**

I felt a warm and cozy feeling come over me and I could not stop crying. I felt something touch my back. I almost looked around to see if there was anybody there. I opened my eyes but there was no one.

Then, I heard these words, "I've got your back and **I AM for you.**"

I can't explain it, but for the first time I felt valuable to someone, that someone cared about me. I knew I didn't have to face this life alone. It's like I had my personal cheerleader saying, "You go, girl, you can do it! I have your back."

This is where I learned to call him, *"My Papa, my Daddy."* Calling him Papa has changed my relationship with him. There is nothing my Papa won't do for me because I am His special child.

God wants all of us to know how much He loves us, and how special we are to Him. He is our greatest Encourager. He is always rooting for us because He knows we will always win. God has happy thoughts toward you every day.

*I have loved you with an everlasting love; I have drawn you with unfailing kindness.* Jeremiah 31:3, NIV

Sit on your Daddy's lap and let Him tell you how special you are to Him. Listen to His word to you.

*My child, on the day you were born, I hovered over you with excitement, knowing my beautiful creation had come to fulfillment. I have always wanted you. You were never a mistake in my eyes. I wanted to show you how much I love to shower you with blessings, grace, and mercy because you are my child, made in my image. Your earthly parents are only stewards of you, but truly, you belong to Me. I desire to have an intimate relationship with you. I am a good Papa. Whatever you need, I will provide — feel free to ask Me. My love for you will never stop, never grow old, and never lose potency. You can always trust me because I am always faithful to you.*

*You may have read in My Word that I rejoice over you with singing. This is true. Open up your ears and heart; you may hear me singing to you. There is nothing more valuable in this universe that I have created, other than you. I am your greatest Fan, your greatest Cheerleader, and your greatest Encourager. I gave up my Son, Jesus, so that I could gain you back. I will never let you go. I want the opportunity for us to get to know each other better.*

*Love, Your Heavenly Father, God Almighty, Your Papa.*

God desires for you to know Him as Father, more than you can comprehend. Pray this prayer to begin your journey now in getting to know "Papa."

## Prayer of Healing

*Papa, I desire to receive Your love for me into my spirit. Remove any roadblocks and hindrances in my heart that would interfere in my receiving this love. Open my ears and eyes to where I have missed seeing and hearing Your love for me. Shower Your love upon me now so that I can know You as my Father. Thank You for the gift of love.*

*In Jesus' Name, Amen.*

## Questions

1. Have you ever experienced the love of God?
2. Have you heard your Heavenly Father call your name?

## Application

1. Meditate on the Scriptures that describe how much God loves you.
2. Go to a quiet place and allow God to speak to your heart.

*"And to know the love of Christ that surpasses knowledge,
that you may be filled with all the full-
ness of God." Ephesians 3:19, ESV.*

*"For God so loved the world that He gave His one and only
Son, that whoever believes in Him shall not
perish but have eternal life." John 3:16, NIV.*

*"For I know the plans I have for you," declares the Lord, "plans
to prosper you and not to harm you, plans to give
you hope and a future." Jeremiah 29:11, NIV*

# Chapter 10

## WHEN YOU ARE REJECTED

I WAS PASSED OVER FOR A ROLE IN A SCHOOL PLAY. MY teacher gave it to her favorite student and I was deeply hurt.

"What was wrong with me?" I asked.

What does rejection look like? It's like having a hole in your bucket.

There's song that goes something like, "There's a hole in my bucket, dear Liza, dear Liza. Well then, fix it dear Henry, dear Henry."

Nothing can stay in a bucket with a hole.

Rejection can be defined as, "To refuse or accept a person. To throw away, discard, or to cast out. To refuse as unsatisfactory."

When we are rejected, we build walls around ourselves to protect ourselves. We don't want people to see our insecurity, loneliness, self-pity, or vanity. We project a negative self-image upon ourselves, become critical, and reject others and ourselves. This cycle of rejection undercuts our relationships with God and others.

No matter how much love we receive, we still do not feel loved. It's like being in a love vacuum because we cannot retain the love we receive. Thus, to compensate for feeling unloved, we fill our lives with such things as possessions, recognition, careers, etc. Some of us go the negative route of becoming pleasure and addiction-seeking.

## Symptoms of Rejection

- Anger
- Aggression
- Hardness
- Competiveness
- Argumentativeness
- Stubbornness
- Rebelliousness
- Passivity
- Development of fear-related issues
- Self-pity
- Inferiorities
- Anxiety
- Depression
- Building walls around yourself, in order to protect yourself from being hurt

These behaviors result in becoming more self-centered and seeking fulfillment in everything other than God.

For a long time, I could not thank God for giving me life. I never wanted to be here. I just didn't appreciate life. I knew I wasn't supposed to feel this way, but I didn't know why I did.

God began to show me that in my mother's womb, I had received a spirit of rejection. My mother had thought that she was through having kids and she just didn't want another child.

It is key to uncover the origins of rejection in one's life. Trauma in the womb (attempted abortion), being an unwanted child, or childhood rejections are examples of where the root of rejection could come from.

Rejection can affect your whole personality. We cannot fully enter an intimate fellowship with God when we are unable to receive His acceptance and love.

There are many kinds of rejections, but one of the most devastating is when you are rejected by someone you care a lot about or someone you think you love. One time, in particular, in high school and the beginning of college, I felt I was in love with a young man and he totally rejected me for someone else.

Being rejected breaks down your sense of your own value. I would often second-guess myself. I went through the process of inner healing, because only God can heal those hurts and seal up the hole in the bucket. He gave me stability and a sense of value in my life. Nothing could fill up that hole except a revelation of God and how much I meant to Him.

Sometimes, women feel that having a man will complete them. But God reminded me that **I am only complete in Him**. A man or marriage does not define my womanhood. **I am a woman by God's design**. God sealed that bucket when I became a daughter of the King.

Spend time allowing God to show you who you still need to forgive. Dealing with rejection has a lot to do with forgiving others.

## Prayer of Healing

*Heavenly Father, I acknowledge that I have built walls of rejection in my life. I desire these walls to come down. I will start this healing process by forgiving those that You bring to my mind. In the name of Jesus, I repent of every sin known and unknown that I have committed, that has allowed the spirit of rejection to take root in my life. I repent of every sin of self-pity, control, and self-centeredness that has allowed this spirit permission to operate. Thank You for the power of the Cross and the blood of Jesus, which sets me free.*

*In Jesus' Name, Amen.*

## Questions

1. Whom do you need to forgive? (Make a list.)
2. Which of the symptoms of rejection do you identify with?
3. What is the root cause of your rejection?

## Application

1. With the names you have listed, pray the *Prayer of Forgiveness* over each name. Forgive and release them to God.

## Prayer of Forgiveness

*Father, You have showed me that healing and freedom comes through forgiveness. I choose to forgive _____ (name) for the _____ (offense). I forgive _____ for the hurt they caused me. I choose to release them from any debt or expectation that I thought they owed me. I let go of all judgment and punishment toward them. Through the power of the blood of Jesus and what He did for me on the Cross, I place them at the foot of the Cross and release them to Jesus. Thank You for the gift of forgiveness.*

*In Jesus' Name, Amen!*

# Chapter 11

## WHEN YOUR DREAMS DIE

*"I AM TOO OLD TO START THIS PROJECT NOW." "I DON'T FEEL capable of doing this."*

Has life taken such a toll on you that you have lost hope for your dreams and visions to be fulfilled? Do you feel that you are in such a deep hole that you can't climb out?

It was my dream to be a teacher and to get a master's degree; I wanted to go as high as I could. I didn't want to have the regret later on of not doing it. But when I failed the Miller Analysis Test, which is necessary for graduate school admission, I lost my self-confidence and the hope of getting a master's degree.

*If I didn't do well on this test, I won't be able to do well in the next test,* I thought to myself.

The failure triggered memories of my SAT scores and made me lack confidence that I could accomplish this. I felt like a failure.

My college professor told me to press on and study in a different way. "Don't disqualify yourself just because you didn't pass this test. You have to learn the procedure of analysis which you are not used to," he said.

He sat down with me and gave me practical study methods. I did the Miller Analysis Test a second time around, and I passed! I qualified for the master's program and I was awarded a fellowship for a master's program in special education at California State University.

*Hope deferred makes the heart sick, but a longing fulfilled is like a tree of life.* Proverbs 13:12, NET

When God gives a dream or a vision, He gives us everything we need to make it happen. Go down memory lane and think about how you were excited when you first conceived this idea. Go back to the place where you let the dream die. We don't have to let present pain drive out our future dreams or allow past failures stop us from walking into our destiny.

## Prayer of Healing

*Father, I thank You that You give Your children dreams and assignments that are bigger than ourselves. Help me to uncover why I lost my dream. Lord, help me deal with the pain associated with the loss of my dream. I thank You that dreams are never lost in You. Show me what practical steps I can take this week to reactivate my dream. Thank You that every day is a new start in You.*

*In Jesus' Name. Amen.*

## Questions

*"For I know the plans I have for you," declares the Lord, "plans to prosper you and not to harm you, plans to give you hope and a future." Jeremiah 29:11, NIV.*

In 2 Kings 6:5-7, someone lost a borrowed axhead in the water. Elisha, the prophet, asked, "Where did it fall?" When he was shown the place, Elisha cut a stick, threw it there, and made the iron float. He told the servant to retrieve his axhead.

Go back to where you lost that dream. Ask yourself:
1. Where did I lose the dream?
2. What was going on in my life at that time?

## Application

1. Write out your dream or vision.

*And the Lord answered me: "Write the vision; make it plain on tablets, so he may run who reads it."*
Habakkuk 2:2, English Standard Version

2. Take practical steps to reactivate that dream.

# Chapter 12

## WHEN WORDS CAN KILL

*"YOU CAN'T TRUST MEN, THEY ARE ALL THE SAME." "I WILL never have a baby." "I can't talk in public." "I'll get even with them if it's the last thing I do." "I will never love anyone like that anymore."*

Words are containers that bring us blessing or curses. *You choose the words to speak life or death.*

## Case 1

Jody (not her real name) was the eldest of five children and her parents had to work all the time. From the tender age of six, Jody had to take care of her siblings like she was the mom. She fed them, bathed them, and cooked for them. Jody grew up resenting her role. She had to be a mom to her siblings until she was eighteen.

"I raised my sisters and brothers. I don't want to have any children," she said to herself. Resentment and bitterness took root in her heart.

Some years later, she got married. After being married for three or four years, she and her husband decided to have kids but she couldn't get pregnant. She went to the doctor, who found nothing biologically wrong with her. She went to a prayer counselor and realized that she had made the vow as a child not to have children. After repenting and renouncing this vow, she was able to have a child.

## Case 2

Angela (not her real name) was sexually molested by her cousins at a young age.

"I will never trust a man," she said to herself.

In her personal life, she went from one relationship to the next. Finally, she did get married but experienced marital problems. She kept secrets from her husband and found it hard to be intimate with him. Angela didn't realize where this was coming from because she had forgiven her offenders.

She went for spiritual counseling and through prayer, she discovered that she had vowed that she would never trust men. When she repented, the vow was broken. After that, she was able to open up to her husband emotionally and intimately.

*Words kill, words give life; they're either poison or fruit—you choose. Proverbs 18:21, MSG.*

The inner vows we make in our childhoods, whether conscious or unconscious, shape our characters, over time. When we make statements accompanied by strong emotions, with an unyielding bitter compromise, they take a foothold in our lives. It makes our hearts hard in that area. These inner vows have been long forgotten, but remain in the invisible realm of our consciousness. The Holy Spirit is the only One who can bring them to the surface.

## Examples of Inner Vows

- I will never ever do_____ .
- They won't get a chance to embarrass me like that again because I will never_____ .
- I'll get even with them if it's the last thing I do.
- I will never write again.

*Do not harden your hearts, as they were hardened once when you provoked me, and put me to the test in the wilderness.* Hebrews 3:8

Inner vows need to be discovered, repented of, and broken. Allow the Holy Spirit to search out your heart, so that you can repent and break their negative effect over your life.

## Prayer of Healing

*Lord, I need Your help to reveal any inner vow I have made that is hindering my life. I give You permission to walk back through my life and find these hidden areas. Let the hidden things be revealed. As You reveal these inner vows I have spoken over myself, I ask for forgiveness and I repent of this sin. I renounce and release the hold the vow has had over my life. I break agreement with this vow and the enemy's influence over my life. Thank You for Your forgiveness and for releasing me from this inner vow.*

*In Jesus' Name, Amen.*

## Questions

1. Has something happened in your life and there is no reasonable explanation for it?
2. Ask the Holy Spirit to unveil any inner vows.

## Application

1. Pray this prayer over each inner vow the Holy Spirit reveals.

## Prayer of Healing and Forgiveness

*(Renouncing Inner Vows)*

*Father, forgive me for speaking the inner vow of _____ over my life, which brought certain curses. I forgive that person _____ (name them) who caused me to make this vow. I renounce this inner vow and the resulting curses. I break the power it has held over my life, through the blood of Jesus and the power of the Cross. Thank You for releasing me from this inner vow. I now receive my freedom in Christ.*

*In Jesus' Name, Amen.*

# Chapter 13

## WHEN YOU HAVE FALLEN
## OFF THE WAGON

WE ALL HAVE SOMETHING IN OUR LIVES THAT WE JUST CAN'T get the victory over. It may not be "big sin" issues; it could be just a habit we can't overcome. These things alone can make us feel like failures.

I have been a professional dieter almost all my adult life. I have lost the weight of at least three people, and gained six people. I have tried every diet that is out there. I have tried juicing and eating correctly. I seem to do well for a while and then I fall off the wagon. This is one area where I have prayed and attempted to do right but honestly, I have failed.

I promised God that I would do better by vowing, "I will never eat like that again." But the key lime pie would somehow jump out of the plate into my mouth, down to my stomach without my consent (smile). There is a reason why I haven't been able to gain freedom in my eating habits. It is because I haven't faced the truth about this area of my life. I am addicted to food!

I have to admit that I love to eat, and I have not surrendered this area to God. I give it to Him and take it back. It's like rolling a ball by pushing it away, and then I run over to the other side and take the ball back.

God will take care of those areas if you submit them to Him.

*Roll your works upon the Lord, commit (and trust them wholly to Him; He will cause your thoughts to become agreeable to His will, and) so shall your plans be established and succeed. Proverbs 16:3, AMP*

I have to admit that when this area stays submitted under God, I find success. God gives us grace each day to start afresh. He doesn't condemn us when we fail.

*There is therefore now no condemnation for those who are in Christ Jesus. Romans 8:1, ESV*

I am finding victory in God, one day at a time.

*If you don't like something — change it; if you can't change it, change the way you think about it.* Mary Engelbreit

Let's truly submit those difficult areas to God and leave them with Him. Get His perspective on what you need to overcome, while focusing on the power of the Cross.

Begin to declare that you are free in that area. Declare the opposite of what you have been saying. In the area of food, for example, instead of saying, "I am addicted to food," say, "I am free to make right choices concerning my diet. I do not overeat."

## Question

1. What are the areas in my life where I keep failing, unable to maintain victory?

## Application

1. Find scriptures that address those areas and meditate on them.
2. Declare these scriptures continually throughout your day.

# Chapter 14

## GETTING RID OF THE SKELETONS IN THE CLOSET

*"YOU ACT LIKE YOUR FATHER SOMETIMES."*

I hated to hear these words each time my mother said them. Whenever I felt I was being attacked, I would make negative, cutting remarks, because I knew it might be true of me.

You may have heard someone say that you look like your grandmother or have characteristics like your Aunt Susie. Just as there are different kinds of inherited genetic or medical disease tendencies, such as heart disease or diabetes, there are also inherited ancestral sins, which is a heart tendency to get involved in certain sins found in your family line. For example, you may find your family members from different generations having the same common issue, such as addictions, divorce, anger, abuse, depression, etc.

What does generational sin look like? It is like walking outside and accidently stepping on dog poop. We try vigorously to wipe it off and we think we have gotten it all off, only to step into the house and find ourselves still smelling of dog poop. This is the residue of sin lingering on you.

An Israeli proverb says, "The parents ate the sour grapes and the children had the bitter taste." In a nutshell, it means that what was permitted in families can still be in effect today if we don't get the right cure.

Just as we can change the condition of our physical bodies by taking control of our health, we can also put an end to the curses of our ancestral line by stopping them in our generation. God does not want us to continually carry sin and He made provision for us to be free. How do we stop it?

## Steps to Stop Generational Sin

1. Acknowledge what the sin is and that you are aware of those tendencies in your bloodline.
2. Recognize that someone must own this sin as his or hers and stand in the gap by confession.
3. Forgive your ancestors for bringing this sin or sins into your family line and forgive yourself for your participation in this sin.
4. Stand against the sin.

*I will not participate with this sin nor have anything to do with it. I break all ties with this from my life and my family's life because of what Jesus did for me on the Cross through His blood.*

## Prayer of Healing

*I confess the sin of _____ (name the sin) of my ancestors or parents and even myself. I forgive and release all those persons who brought this sin into my bloodline including myself. I renounce, break, and turn away from this sin of _____ (name the sin) for myself, and my*

*family, because of the Cross and Jesus' shed blood. By faith I receive freedom from the sins and curses surrounding them.*
   *In Jesus' Name, Amen.*

## Questions

1. What sin do you see recurring over and over in your family?
2. What sin do you see recurring in your life over and over, which you feel comes from some generational curse?

## Application

1. Write out a list of each sin occurring in your family line and in your life.
2. Go through the Prayer of Healing for each one of these sins.

# Chapter 15

## WHEN YOU CAN'T GO
## ON ANYMORE

"I CAN'T GO ON, LORD. I HAVE HAD ENOUGH," I SAID TO myself one Sunday evening. I placed a bottle of sleeping pills in front of me as I sat on my bed.

I had been depressed for several months. I was extremely stressed working in my job and I was upset with God that I was still single. I was already in my thirties and still had not married. My hopes and dreams were dashed.

For several months, I went through the motions of going to church every Sunday and serving Him in full-time ministry, but I felt that my life was going in a direction that I had no control over. I felt hopeless and all alone in this world. I was ashamed and didn't talk to anyone because I felt family and friends wouldn't understand.

I just wanted to go to sleep and not wake up in pain anymore. I cried out to God to take away my pain.

*I waited and waited and waited for God. At last he looked;
finally he listened. He lifted me out of the ditch, pulled
me from deep mud. He stood me up on a solid rock to
make sure I wouldn't slip. Psalms 40:1-2, MSG.*

During this time, God reminded me that I have an enemy, Satan, who would love to get credit for cutting my life short. But God showed me that my life was greater than my present circumstances, and that what I was experiencing *now* did not determine my *future*.

Life isn't always fair, but God is just. I didn't have the last say-so over my life, He did, and my future was blessed. **God began to speak life into my destiny, to give me hope.**

*The days of my life [were] all prepared before I'd even lived
one day. Psalms 139:16, MSG*

*"For I know the plans I have for you," declares the Lord, "plans
to prosper you and not to harm you, plans to give
you hope and a future." Jeremiah 29:11, NIV*

## Prayer of Healing

*Father, I thank You that You are showing me that I am not without hope. Hope says that there is always the expectation of good coming to me. Lord, Your good surrounds me like a shield. Lord, help me to remember You are the only one that has the authority to give and take life. Forgive me for not honoring Your authority as I consider taking matters into my own hands. Show me the wonderful destiny and plans You have for me.*

*In Jesus' Name, Amen.*

## Questions

1. Have you ever felt hopeless — that you could not go on?

2. Have you isolated yourself from friends and family?
3. Do you feel you could go to sleep and not wake up?
4. Are you constantly depressed, feeling helpless, worthless, angry, or guilty?

## Application

1. If you have any of these feelings for more than one to two months, seek out professional help.
2. Find someone you can talk with in confidence (e.g., your pastor, family member, or a good friend).
3. Take a moment and remember all the great things that have happened in your life so far.
4. Psalm 139 says that before you were born, God made great plans for your life. So write out some of the things that you feel He may have in store for you.
5. One of the greatest gifts God has given us is laughter. The Bible says laughter is like medicine. So look at a funny movie, read some jokes or talk with friends about some of their funny stories or your own funny stories.

# Chapter 16

## TRYING TO HELP GOD OUT

SOCIETY TELLS US, "TO BE COMPLETE, WE NEED A MATE." WE desire a mate because as women, our desire is to have someone to love and to be loved in return. We want a family because we derive our identity through relationships. The closest earthly relationship that we can have is between a husband and wife.

I found myself being desperate because time had passed me by and I was no longer of the age to bear children. When my husband-to-be came into my life, I was so excited about getting married that I ignored my own principle about marriage counseling. I was more concerned with the idea of getting married than the person I was marrying. I had always said that I would go through pre-marital counseling, but I didn't. I ignored the warning signs such as his financial instability, his many previous marriages, and counsel from close friends. I was looking at my husband-to-be through rose-colored glasses.

I was elated at the chance to get married since I was no "spring chicken." I tried to cover over our differences and spiritualize our union by saying we would be able to work together in the ministry. I was so caught up with the idea of getting married that I stopped focusing on building the relationship. I lied to myself, saying that some of our incompatibilities were very little and we could overcome them through prayer. But I was really more in love with the idea of marriage than with my spouse-to-be.

In the beginning we were happy and tried hard to make it work because we did not want to disappoint God. I didn't realize that I had missed the major road signs and the hard fact that he was not the right person for me, and neither was I the right person for him. My mother had great reservations about us getting married but she didn't want to interfere in my life. Needless to say, this marriage did not have a good start as both of us were in deception about each other.

You might be saying, "You prayed and you still missed the mark." Yes, I saw only what I wanted to see. God does not take away our free will. We are not infallible, only God is.

Do not be in a hurry to marry someone just because you feel the biological clock is ticking. It is better to be single and happy than to be married and unhappy.

God does not need our help. His plan is to give you a future and a hope. Give God all the time He needs to bring that person to you. Don't allow the devil to trick you into thinking that the grass is greener on the other side. With the wrong person, it is like living in weeds. Life is not over; there is still time for God to fulfill His promise to you.

## Prayer of Healing

*Father, forgive me for not trusting You enough to bring the right man/woman into my life. I ask for Your forgiveness for all the times I have tried to fulfill getting a mate through my own efforts and agenda. Today, I decide I will not go ahead of You, just like Sarah did in the Bible when she gave her maid-servant Hagar to Abraham that produced the child Ishmael. I will take hold of the promise in Isaiah 34:16 that You will send the right mate for me. By faith, I thank You for providing my mate.*

Seek out of the book of the Lord and read: not one of these [details of prophecy] shall fail; none shall want and lack her mate [in fulfillment], for the mouth [of the Lord] has commanded, and His Spirit has gathered them. Isaiah 34:16 (AMP).

If God is concerned about bringing mates for his creation, how concerned He must be about bringing a mate for you, His most valuable creation.

## Questions

1. Do you have any relationships with the opposite sex that are not healthy for you?
2. If you are single, are you controlling your sexual desires by avoiding fornication?
3. Have you given God the right to have the final say in this area of your life?

## Application

1. Spend time alone with God and allow Him to speak to you about this area of your life. Share with Him your feelings of disappointment, loneliness, and anger. Let Him bring you comfort from His Word.
2. Share with God what you would like in a mate. Bring this list to Him and see what God has to say about it. Don't be afraid to trust Him in this area.

# Chapter 17

## WHEN THE HURT DOESN'T GO AWAY

When my husband left me, I felt a deep and hurting loss...

All of us can remember a hurt that was so devastating that we seemed to be unable to shake it. Sometimes, the hurt just doesn't seem to go away. We have done all we know to do. We have taken all the steps and prayed all the prayers, but still the hurt continues every time we think about it.

After my husband left me, I couldn't get myself together and I went into depression. One day, I drove out of the garage with the automatic door still closed. I almost crashed through the metal door and broke the garage door opener. That was when I realized that I needed help. I went to the doctor to get pills to help me to focus, but that didn't help; it only gave me a big stomachache.

Grief has its seasons. Even though I knew the process of inner healing, I needed help. I went to a professional Christian counselor to deal with the feelings of hurt, anger, and loneliness. Through consistent prayer counseling, I was able to get relief and the help I needed.

If the hurt has consumed you and has taken over your life, it is time you seek out help. We are not placed on this earth to be by ourselves. From time to time, we need to get the right kind of help from others who can guide us over these difficulties.

> *Confess your sins to one another and pray for one another, that you may be healed. James 5:16, ESV*

Sin may be wrong thoughts or ungodly beliefs that you hold concerning the situation. Sometimes we are so close to our present situation that we aren't able to get a clear perspective on it and we need professional help. You might consider going to your pastor, counselor, therapist, or life coach.

## Prayer of Healing

*Father, help me to be honest with You and with myself. This pain is too much for me to bear alone. Let me not hide my pain any longer. Let me recognize when I need help.*

*Please lead me to someone who can help me walk through this. Your Word tells me that You will direct and guide me by Your Spirit, therefore I trust You to direct me to that person.*

*In Jesus' Name, thank You for meeting my need. Amen.*

## Questions

1. Has this pain/hurt persisted for more than one or two months?
2. Is this pain/hurt consuming all of your time?
3. Have you done all you can but the pain/hurt still persists?

If you have answered, "yes" to all of the above questions, you may need professional help. Here's a resource list for you to consider in getting the help you need.

## Resources

1. Cleansing Stream: www.cleansingstream.org:
2. Restoring: the: Foundations: www.rtfi.org
3. Elijah: House: www.elijahhouse.org:
4. Ellel: Ministries: www.ellelministries.org
5. Sozo: Ministries: www.bethelsozo.com

# Chapter 18

## LEAVING THE PAST BEHIND

"*IF YOU DON'T DO THIS NOW YOU MAY NEVER DO IT,*" *I TOLD myself. I knew it was time for me to move on and take a step of faith.*

It is hard to leave the known and familiar for the unknown, even when we know what we are holding onto is blocking the future.

It was time for me to resign from my job and start my own ministry. My heart had already moved on from the place where I presently was but my body continued to be there, going through all the physical motions. It was difficult to leave a job that gave me a salary and to start raising my own support from scratch.

I had wanted to stay in my comfort zone, even though I knew I could not fulfill the dream God gave me. God did me a favor by leading my heart out first, so that it would be easier for me to follow physically.

God is always moving us forward into greater areas of our destiny, but when we stop to build a monument to our pasts, it holds us back from focusing on our futures.

*Brothers, I do not consider that I have made it my own. But one thing I do; forgetting what lies behind and straining forward to what lies ahead. Philippians 3:13, ESV*

No matter how difficult our past was, we sometimes cling on to it and refuse to let it go. It could be a dead-end job, a failed marriage, a hurtful childhood, or an abusive relationship.

*Forget about what's happened; don't keep going over old history. Be alert — be present. I'm about to do something brand-new. It's bursting out! Don't you see it? Isaiah 43:18-19, MSG*

Let's not carry the past around like excess baggage. Let's learn our life lessons from the past and move on. God wants to give a fresh sheet of paper to write a new future, and not to rewrite the old past.

> *Letting go doesn't mean giving up...it means moving on. It is one of the hardest things a person can do. Starting at birth, we grasp on to anything we can get our hands on, and hold on as if we will cease to exist when we let go. We feel that letting go is giving up, quitting, and that, as we all know, is cowardly. But as we grow older we are forced to change our way of thinking. We are forced to realize that letting go means accepting things that cannot be. It means maturing and moving on, no matter how hard you have to fight yourself to do so. — Unknown*

*Has this world been so kind to you that you should leave with regret? There are better things ahead than any we leave behind.* — C. S. Lewis

*When one door closes, another opens, but often we look so long at the closed door that we do not see the one that has been opened for us.* — Helen Keller

God has a wonderful plan for our life! Go; take the plunge to move out from your past and into your destiny. Say good-bye to the past! Even if you are afraid, do it anyway.

*I have it all planned out — plans to take care of you, not abandon you, plans to give you the future you hope for. Jeremiah 29:11, MSG*

## Prayers

*Heavenly Father, help me to be bold enough to put my past behind me so that I can step into my hopeful future with You. Show me the lessons that my past held so that I can learn from them as well as avoid the same pitfalls. Thank You for loving me so much that You are committed to seeing me fulfill my destiny.*

*In Jesus' Name, Amen.*

## Questions

1. What do you need to leave behind in order to be released from your past?
2. What are your biggest challenges in letting go?

## Application

1. List three steps you can make today that would help you move forward into the future.

# Chapter 19

## LEARNING HOW TO BLESS

NOW THAT WE HAVE COME TO THE CONCLUSION OF THIS book, I want to share with you about how you can speak blessing over your life and others. Finally, I want to speak blessing over you.

Can you ever remember a time in your life when someone spoke words of encouragement over your life that sent you into the realm of positive and new direction?

I have a friend, John Dawson, whom I have known for over thirty years. He has always spoken blessings over my life. John has encouraged me in such a way that his words penetrate into my heart and spirit. His words of encouragement have helped to propel me into my destiny.

God wants us to speak blessings over our lives as well as over those of other people. When we bless others, it helps to strengthen our spirit and propel us toward our destiny.

God spoke to Abram in Genesis 12:2-3b, *And I will make you a great nation, and I will bless you and make your name great, so that you will be a blessing…and in you, all the families of the earth shall be blessed.*

God wants us to continue these ancestral blessings in our family line. If you speak blessings over your children, it sets their destiny just as Isaac blessed Jacob, and Jacob blessed his sons.

As a Prayer Minister in the Life Transformation sessions, one of the things I do is to stand as a representative of the person's parent and pronounce a blessing over his or her life. It is never too late to receive a parental blessing.

Get in the practice of speaking blessings over your life until it becomes a habit, and you will naturally speak it over others.

## Prayer

*Father, I know that You have pronounced blessing over my life. Help me to learn how to declare the blessings from Your Word and personalize them to my life. Now I determine to be a blessing wherever I go. Thank You for blessing me to be a blessing.*

*In Jesus' Name, Amen.*

## Questions

1. Has anyone blessed you like this in your life? (Name each person and the blessing.)
2. Is there anyone you would like to bless?

## Application

1. Thank each person who has blessed you.
2. Write out your own personal prayer of blessing.
Let me speak a prayer of blessing over you.

> *I speak blessings to your spirit in the name of Jesus Christ. Listen with your spirit in the*

*name of Jesus. The Word of God says that you are blessed coming in and going out. I bless you to experience the privileges of being a beloved child of God, believing His promises for your life. I bless you to take hold of God's supernatural strength to focus your attention on what is good, honest, just, and lovely.*

*God has blessed you with the ability to walk in wholeness, giving you the opportunity to overcome temptation and become more than a conqueror. I bless you in knowing what your loving Father has destined you to become and do in His Kingdom.*

*I bless you in understanding that God is your biggest cheerleader and all your circumstances will be used for good in your life. May God bless your home with peace and give you success and prosperity in your job and business. I bless you to be able to fulfill your dreams and visions. May goodness and mercy follow you all the days of your life. The Lord bless you and keep you. The Lord make His face shine upon you and be gracious unto you. The Lord lift up His countenance upon you and give you peace.*

*I bless you in Jesus' Name.*

Now speak this blessing over your life and find someone else to speak this blessing to. You will extend a bridge of blessing to everyone you meet.

CPSIA information can be obtained
at www.ICGtesting.com
Printed in the USA
FFOW03n0740231015
17907FF

9 781460 241226